maker.

maker.

Home

THIS IS A CARLTON BOOK

Published by Carlton Books Ltd
20 Mortimer Street
London W1T 3JW

Text Copyright © 2019 Carlton Books Limited

Design Copyright © 2019 Carlton Books Limited

ISBN 978 1 78739 251 9

Editorial: Issy Wilkinson
Design: Russell Knowles, Luana Gobbo
Production: Marion Storz
Photography: Tobias George

A CIP catalogue for this book is available from the British Library

10 9 8 7 6 5 4 3 2 1

Printed in Dubai

maker.

Tobias George.

Home

15 Step-by-step Projects to Transform Your
Home Using Everyday Materials

CARLTON
BOOKS

maker.

Home

Contents

01. Storage block

A simple project to get started. Using offcuts to create a neat storage block for your desk, and an easily adaptable design to make a single stem planter.

02. Wine glass holder

A great-looking piece made using basic tools. A super easy-to-make gift idea.

03. Chopping or serving board

A solid wood board to be used in the kitchen for chopping, or for stylishly displaying and serving food. An opportunity to develop your wood-finishing skills.

04. Copper stand

Use various lengths of copper pipe to create a simple alternative stand for books and electric tablets. Affordable and chic, the techniques you pick up in this make can be applied to larger and more complex projects later on.

05. Boot holder

Made with 100 per cent reclaimed timber, this boot holder will instantly tidy up your entrance hall or porch, keeping muddy boots in their place.

06. Wooden scoop

A hand-carved wooden scoop, ideal for coffee beans or other dry goods. Made with traditional tools and techniques to give a unique, handmade finish.

07. Milking stool

A new take on a traditional three-legged milking stool. Working with solid wood and hand-whittling legs, the skills you use can be transferred to similar but scaled-up makes later on.

08. Wall-mounted tool storage

An adaptable piece to keep all your tools organized and in one place – exactly what you need now you've embarked on your making journey.

09. Concrete planter

Experimenting with an on-trend and versatile material, this planter will add a modern industrial look to any room and brings greenery into the home.

10. Magnetic knife-holder

Off-cuts from the timber pile have so many uses, and this is just one of them. Create a functional, standout piece for your kitchen.

11. Weaving loom

My take on a traditional weaving loom, using high-quality timber to ensure this product will last but also look great. A project that will encourage and inspire even more making.

12. Coffee table

Hard-wearing joints create a solid, everyday piece. Building it yourself is building it to last, and this coffee table will become an instant classic.

13. Bookshelf

A shelving unit to store all sorts of bits and pieces in your home. Once you get the hang of the skills used here, you can progress to making larger bookshelves and other pieces.

14. Clothes rail

Scandinavian style inspires this beautifully simple and well-designed alternative to clothes storage. Deceptively simple yet impressive.

15. Steam box and lamp

The final and most complex project, broken down into three parts. Learn how to make a steam box, form for moulding your wood and finally a lamp using this traditional, time-honoured technique.

Introduction

Nature has always had a place in my heart. From a young age I've loved the joy that being outside brings and the freedom it gives. My love for the outdoors, coupled with good design and craftsmanship, is something I will eternally be grateful for. The people who have introduced creativity into my life, and those who have taught me invaluable lessons on patience and good craftsmanship, are some of the most important people I have surrounded myself with. If you want to progress with anything in life, find and surround yourself with people who champion you and speak life and light into your world.

I have always carried a love of design and making. As a child, I used to love drawing and sketching, and as I grew up I would often find myself outside in the garden with my dad, or in my grandfather's workshop. Through school I found myself doing particularly well in the more practical subjects, rather than typically academic ones. I always found the school system a little strange, though – encouraging people to work hard and study harder to become as accomplished as possible in academic subjects. It was tricky for me to keep up. But when I was left to my own devices in the more practical subjects, I would find myself stunted by the system, often being told that I wasn't doing things to the curriculum, and that if I wanted to pass, I would have to show I was capable when it came to the academic side of the practical subjects. I appreciate the importance of what the school system was trying to teach me, but I always felt like it didn't matter how talented or skilled you were: if you weren't writing the right things and learning the way you were "supposed" to, then you wouldn't make it to the end of the year with a pass.

The truth is that I learn by doing. I always have done. Having the freedom to explore something in detail, to dismantle it in my own time and have a good look at it is the way I have developed my skills and been able to grow what I do. Spending this time with myself and spending valuable time with my father and grandfather – both when I was younger and even now – has taught me important skills and lessons in the craft. My business began from a place of boredom. Finding myself in unemployment a year after leaving school, I decided to pick up some timber I found at home and make a few pieces. I had no intention of selling anything – I was making purely for the sense of joy and accomplishment you get when you create something with your hands. This quickly became the main reason for starting my business – I absolutely loved the feeling of fulfilment schieved by making. Now reaching the five-year mark, I still get this feeling everyday: complete and utter job satisfaction from making something that is going to be used, loved and treasured.

As my skillset has progressed and I've grown as a maker I've had some important revelations. Natural materials often start and end, just like everything in life, but if we can prolong the end of something natural, then we must do what we can. The thought of a material like wood being used to its fullest potential, for as many years as possible, brings me so much joy. It's why I have a passion for reusing and recycling. Taking a material or piece of furniture that has been used for many years as one thing, and having the skill to restore it – or even totally dismantle it but reuse each piece for a new season of its life, bringing joy to someone as a totally different product – is so exciting to me.

In an age where people are becoming so much more aware of the impact humanity has had – and is having – on our planet, we are doing everything we can to prevent further damage. We are conscious of where our clothes come from and how they are produced. We are far more aware of where our food is coming from and the impact its production is having on the planet. But for some reason it still feels like we are trailing behind when it comes to things we are putting in our homes. We are so quick to take a trip to these huge affordable home stores – a rite of passage when we get our own space – to stock up on poor-quality furniture and an abundance of other bits and pieces that we often don't need.

As my business has developed, and I have progressed from making small home décor pieces to larger, higher-quality pieces of furniture, I always hear the same thing from my customers: that a couple or individual has moved into their first place and have made the ritualistic run to one of these affordable furniture warehouse stores to gather as much stuff as possible to fill their space, but after two or three years these products have either not lasted, or the initial joy at finding cheap products has turned into a desire to own higher-quality pieces. Pieces that will stand the test of time, and will continue to do so for many years to come. Pieces that change and develop with everyday use and family life, to the point where they almost become part of the family. Pieces covered in marks and scratches that hold their own stories and memories from years and years of use and fulfilment. I don't claim to achieve this with every product I make – I've realized that sometimes I do just need to create a functional, affordable piece for a customer in order to meet their requirements and also to earn a living for myself – but even with these simple pieces its crucial for me to produce something that will last. It may not have been produced using the highest-quality materials or the most advanced woodworking techniques, but I will always ensure that it will last. And, for me, this is the most important thing. With anything from a chopping board or wooden spoon, to a coffee table or built-in wardrobe, it doesn't matter how it's been created or what techniques have been used, as long as it lasts and ages well. I once heard the quote, "The memory of poor quality lasts longer than the brief delight in its low price." Those words have stuck with me as I have built and grown my creative business.

Throughout this book you will have the opportunity to learn new skills, develop those skills and hopefully gain the confidence to create something beautiful for your home. Whatever it is you make, you will always be able to hold onto the fact that *you* made it. There are no templates for the products in this book, and there are very few measurements to stick to; this is to ensure that whatever is produced is totally unique, bespoke and made by the user to be as functional in their everyday life as possible. Some of the earlier projects in this book are very simple, then they get progressively more difficult, using skills and techniques that will hopefully stretch your skillset and help you to produce something you're proud of yourself for making – and that will improve your home in a way that a mass-produced product would never be able to.

Project
01.
Storage block

If you're anything like me, you'll likely have a bunch of wood knocking about that's too good to burn, but too small or insignificant to use on a larger project. This project is a great way to use up any leftover wood from previous jobs.

Tools & Materials

Tools:

- Drill bits (various sizes)
- Electric sander and sandpaper
- Saw
- Ruler or tape measure
- White or coloured masking tape
- Drill

Materials:

- Any square-ish offcuts of wood

Step 1:
Choose wood

Find a suitable piece of wood – ideally it'll be a square piece, of any length. I used a piece of ash I found in my wood pile, but I could've used some oak or a block of sycamore.

Step 2:
Cut

Using your saw, cut your piece of wood to your desired length. I cut mine to about 150 mm (5.9 in) so it's a nice height to keep at one of the work stations in my workshop, holding a couple of pens and pencils within arm's reach.

Step 3: Mark lines

Taking your ruler and pencil, mark a couple of points in from the edge of your block and connect them with a straight pencil line.

This is one of the lines you'll be drilling your holes along, so make sure you mark far enough in from the edge to fit your drill bit.

Repeat this step once or twice more, depending on whether your wood is wide enough to fit a couple of rows of holes.

Step 4: Mark holes

Next lay your ruler along your line and make marks for where you want to drill the holes.

Be sure to space them evenly and bear in mind what you'll stand up in the holes when your project is finished – you'll need to make sure there's enough space for any overhang if you're storing wider objects like scissors.

Step 5: Choose drill bits

Now pick different drill bits to give you options for what you can use the storage block for.

I went for three sizes – 10 mm (0.39 in), 18 mm (0.7 in), and 32 mm (1.2 in).

Step 6: Drill

Clamp your wood to the pillar drill to keep it nice and secure, then start drilling. A pillar drill keeps everything nice and straight, but you can use a hand drill for this.

Step 7: Check depth

To keep the smaller holes the same depth, put a bit of tape around the drill bit at the desired depth.

Keep an eye on the tape as you drill your hole and when it touches the wood, pull the drill bit up. Repeat the process with the next hole.

Step 8: Sand

Give the whole block a good sand down with your electric sander, or sand by hand. You can also take a small bit of sand paper and get into the holes to clean them out.

Step 9: Finish

When it's all sanded, give it a good blow to get rid of any dust. You can either give it a coat of oil or leave it natural, then fill it with whatever fits!

Variation:
Test tube planter

You can use and adapt the steps above to easily create another item – the test tube planter. It's an item that looks great in any home and you can create it for very little cost and effort.

As well as what's needed for the storage block, you'll need:

- 16 mm (0.62 in) drill bit
- 16 mm (0.62 in) Pyrex test tubes

Step 1: Choose wood

Simply grab a block of wood of any shape or size. I used a rectangular block, but the beauty of this project is that you can make a totally unique product with whatever timber you have knocking about.

Step 2: Measure and mark

Measure and make pencil marks at equal points on your block of wood. I usually measure an equal distance from either side for the first two marks, then make another mark in the middle of those.

After that, check the width of the block is enough for your drill bit, and draw a centre line through each of your previous marks.

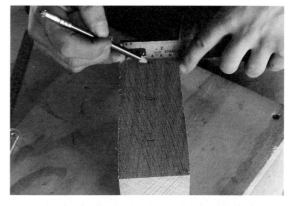

Step 3: Check depth

Like the storage block, you'll want to ensure the holes are the same depth. Measure a suitable depth for your test tubes and mark your drill bit with some tape.

I used a 16 mm (0.62 in) drill bit because that's the size of my test tubes.

Step 4: Sand and finish

Repeat the sanding and finishing steps and pop your test tubes into the holes.

Tip:

These storage blocks are useful to have around the home and workshop, handy for holding all sorts, from stationery to drill bits to tooth-brushes – basically anything that can fit in the holes you drill!

Project
02.
Wine glass holder

Another great project for upcycling offcuts. This wine glass and bottle holder is ideal for getting out on a date night or special occasion, or to give as a simple handmade gift.

Tools & Materials

Tools:

- Handsaw or jigsaw
- Tape measure or ruler
- Drill
- 32 mm (1.2 in) drill bit
- Electric sander (optional) and sandpaper
- Wood file

Materials:

- Length of timber, ideally no thicker than 20 mm (0.78 in) and no longer than 300 mm (11.8 in)

Tip:

Be sure to get this initial centre line as close to the middle as possible. This will prevent the whole thing from sitting crooked on the bottle, which may result in the glasses sliding off.

Step 1: Draw

For this particular project I'm using an oak offcut from a pile of floorboards given to me from a house near my workshop. It's nice to be giving it a new lease of life. To begin, take your tape measure or ruler to measure the width of your piece of wood and draw a line down the centre.

Step 2:
Measure

Next take one of the wine glasses you'll be using and measure the width of the stem. Halve that measurement, then transfer the halved measurement to either side of your centre line. For example, my glass stem was 12 mm (0.47 in) wide, so that's a 6 mm (0.23 in) mark either side of my centre line.

Step 3: Check spacing

At this early point it's worth just placing all three components – a wine bottle and two glasses – on your wood to make sure they fit. By doing this you'll be sure there's enough space between the glasses and the bottle, so they won't bash together when your holder is done. While the glasses and bottle are on your wood, grab a pencil and make a mark roughly in the middle of where each wine glass base stands on the wood.

Step 4: Drill wine bottle hole

Take your ruler and make a mark in the middle of your wood, on the centre line. Take the 32 mm (1.2 in) drill bit – this should be big enough for most wine bottle necks, but if your bottle is a little bigger, then just use a slightly larger drill bit. Put the point of the drill bit on your pencil mark and start drilling carefully through your timber. When the point from the drill bit comes through the other side of your wood, flip the wood around and drill again from the back. This will ensure there's no blow-out of the grain from drilling all the way through. A blow-out, or tear-out, is when a blade or drill bit comes out of a cut and the wood fibres are torn, leaving a splintered edge.

Step 5: Drill wine glass holes

After this you'll need a drill bit the same width (or as close to the width) of your wine glass stem. Drill through the pencil mark you made on your wood for your glasses in Step 3. Drill through these points until the drill bit pops through, and be sure to flip the wood as before.

Step 6:
Cut

Using your saw or jigsaw, cut from both ends along the pencil lines you drew, so the cuts meet the wine glass holes you've just drilled, creating a curved slot into which you can slide your wineglasses.

Step 7:
File and sand

With a relatively smooth file, start filing anywhere you've cut or drilled until the saw marks and drill marks are gone. You can then move onto a piece of sandpaper – I'd recommend around 120 grit for a nice, smooth finish. Then, using your sander with the same grit paper, give the whole piece of wood a good sand down, leaving a nice smooth finish all over.

Project
03.
Chopping
or serving board

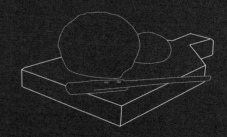

I'm using some nice solid oak for my chopping board – it's an offcut, so has a couple of different lengths to it. I'm opting to use the shorter length at the top as a handle, then cut the longer piece into two for the main part of the board.

Tools & Materials

Tools:

- Long clamps
- Saw
- Plane
- Electric sander (optional)
- Sandpaper (80, 120 and 180 grit)
- Chisel
- Set square

Materials:

- Oak board, 30–50 mm
  (1.18–1.96 in) thick,
  200 mm (7.87 in) wide,
  1 m (3 ft 2 in) long
- Wood glue

Step 1:
Measure and cut

Firstly, if your board has any holes in it, like mine, you'll need to fill it. I drilled a slightly larger hole so I had a perfect circle to work with, then grabbed an offcut of oak and a knife to carve a little wooden plug. I then glued this in, cut it flush and roughly sanded it down.

Next, we'll make a basic board with our cut pieces, which we'll shape and refine later into the finished item. The shape of this initial, rough board doesn't matter too much. The main thing is that we have a large enough piece of wood to work with and later cut into our desired shape.

You'll want to mark your timber before you cut it to length. Simply take your tape measure and measure out your timber into three roughly equal lengths (approx. 330 mm (12.9 in) if your initial piece of oak was 1 m (3 ft 2 in) in length). Using your set square, draw a straight line from your mark to ensure your cut will be nice and straight.

Step 2: Square up

Clamp the wood against your workbench or tighten it in your vice. Using your smoothing plane, square up the edges in preparation for being glued.

Take small amounts off, regularly stopping to check for square edges.

If you're using new timber, then you can probably get away with skipping this step. Just double-check that the edges are square before skipping.

Step 3: Check

Make sure you're happy with your fit by laying your pieces of wood on the workbench. Press them together as they will be when a finished item and ensure there are no gaps between.

Step 4:
Glue

Now apply an even, generous amount of wood glue. Spread it out using a scrap piece of wood.

The board will need washing and wiping down after use, so to prevent it coming apart, remember to use waterproof glue.

Step 5:
Dry

Clamp your wood together with some long clamps. It's also worth clamping your wood down to your workbench or flat surface to keep it flat during the drying process.

Use a damp rag to wipe away any excess glue. This will save a clean-up job in the future.

Leave it to dry for 24 hours.

Step 6: Plane

After 24 hours you can take off the clamps. You should now be left with a nice, solid chunk of wood to work with.

Using your plane, slowly begin to shave off any uneven spots and flatten your board.

Step 7:
Shape

Once you're happy that the board is reasonably flat, you can mark out the shape of your final product.

Clamp the piece down and, using a jigsaw, cut out the shape, being careful to stick to your pencil lines.

Step 8: Sand

When your final shape is cut out and you're happy with it, grab your electric sander or sandpaper and begin sanding. This will both flatten and smooth out any imperfections in your board. I'm using an orbital sander for this process and starting with coarse 80-grit sandpaper.

Step 9: Bevel

Now grab a sharp chisel and run it along the edges of the board to create a bevelled effect.

For this step, it's worth starting on the underside of your board, so you can get the hang of the technique where it's less visible, or even practise beforehand on an offcut.

Use both hands to grip the chisel around the handle and the blade. This will give you a better level of control. There are plenty of videos online on how to safely use chisels.

Step 10: Finish

Give the whole board another sand down, maybe passing the sand-paper over your bevels once or twice to ensure they are even along the edges. Start with 80-grit sandpaper again, and work your way up to 120, then 180.

Between each level of sandpaper, pour some water over the board and wait for it to dry. By soaking the board you'll cause the tiny, stringy fibres to rise up and create a rough, fuzzy feel over the board.

Sand these fibres back down using a finer paper, then repeat this step until the fibres no longer stand up. By doing this now, you'll stop fibres rising once you've oiled and used your board.

Finishing tip:

When it comes to finishes for my boards and spoons, I have always used a home-made balm made by melting coconut oil and beeswax. Have a look in the resource section at the end of the book to find out how to make this.

Step 11: Oil

Use a clean, dry cloth to apply oil or salve to finish the board.

Project
04.
Copper stand

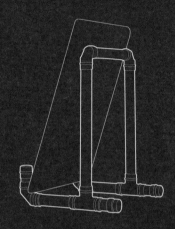

Made from lengths of new or recycled copper, this stand is a great contemporary way to display your electronic tablet or makes a handy stand for books and magazines, especially when you're hard at work in the kitchen.

Tools & Materials

Tools:

- Pipe cutter
- White chalk or marker pen (fine tip)
- Tape measure or ruler
- Blowtorch
- Flux paste
- Wire wool or coarse scouring pad
- Heatproof solder or brazing mat

Materials:

- Length of 15 mm (0.59 in) copper tube, usually sold in 2 m or 3 m (6 ft 5 in or 9 ft 9 in) lengths
- 4 x 15 mm (0.59 in) solder ring elbows
- 2 x 15 mm (0.59 in) solder ring equal tee
- 4 x 15 mm (0.59 in) solder ring stop ends

Step 1: Clean

Ensure your pipes are nice and clean. Grab a bit of wire wool or your scouring pad and give the pipe a rub down. If you're using an older pipe or a piece that's been sitting around for a while, you'll see the layer of dirt come right up and reveal a nice shiny surface.

Step 2: Measure

With the tape measure or ruler, measure the height and width of your tablet or book, and note the measurements down.

Be aware that the copper fittings may add length to your pieces. To deal with this, it's worth cutting your pipes a little short. I found that taking 20 mm (0.78 in) off each end of the pipe does the trick.

For a standard-sized stand suitable for most books, magazines and larger tablets, I cut my pipes to the following measurements: 140 mm (5.5 in), 2 x 180 mm (7 in), 2 x 75 mm (2.9 in), 4 x 30 mm (1.1 in).

Follow this guide or adjust the measurements you've already taken. Measure on your copper pipe where to make your first cut and mark the position with your chalk pen or marker pen.

Step 3: Cut

Use your pipe cutter to cut through the pipe. Simply place the blade of the cutter on your pen mark and tighten the thread with the rollers on. Be sure to not over-tighten.

Start spinning the cutter around the pipe – as it gets easier to spin, tighten the rollers again and continue spinning. After a few moments your pipe should pop off into two pieces.

Repeat the process for all your pieces.

Step 4: Check

When everything is cut, it's worth fitting the stand together to check it's all suitable and holds your desired item.

Give all the pipes another rub with your wire wool and grab the first two pieces you're going to connect together. I used the top bar and one of the side pieces.

Apply a generous amount of flux paste to the ends of both of the pieces of pipe that you want to put the connector on. (The flux cleans the copper even more to allow a better chance of the copper and solder binding together.)

Step 5: Solder

A: First connection

Now lay your pieces flat on the soldering mat on your workbench. Make sure they're at a right angle. It's easy for them to be slightly off without you noticing, and this might stop your final product fitting together.

Grab your blowtorch and begin heating the copper around your connector. The copper isn't too thick, so you won't need a violent flame from your blowtorch; just a gentle heat should do.

Direct the flame towards the connector piece and heat around the solder rings. After a couple of moments, you'll see the flux bubble, and not long after that the solder will begin to appear from the joints. Take the heat away from the joint and, using a wet rag, clean around the freshly soldered pieces, being sure to remove any flux. Be aware that the metal will be very hot, so be careful.

Don't put too much pressure on yourself with this – the process can take a little while to get right, but once mastered becomes second nature. There's no water running through these pipes, so as long as they hold together and they're fairly neat then that's great.

B: Second vertical

Repeat the previous step with the next vertical piece of copper for your stand.

Be sure to measure the distance between the two verticals before soldering, to make sure it's the same at the top and bottom.

If you find it's slightly off afterwards, you can apply a little pressure and bend the joint a little, but you have to be very careful to not bend your copper pipe.

C: Remaining pieces

Continue the soldering step with the other pieces. Be really careful not to heat the rings of solder without a piece of copper in them. If you do, the solder will melt and it'll be tricky to use the rings to connect your copper pipe when you're ready to. (You can see in the photo that the equal tee has three solder rings, so I'll be connecting three pieces of copper together.)

For the perfect finish

Soldering the copper to the connectors is a permanent process, so it's important to double-check everything as you go. Stop to measure everything after you make each connection and after you solder.

Also be sure to give your copper a good wipe down after each step, first with a wet rag then a dry rag. Leaving the flux can result in your copper going a greeny-blue colour. This can be cleaned again with warm water and a rag, but it's good practice to keep them nice and clean throughout each step of the project.

Project
05.
Boot holder

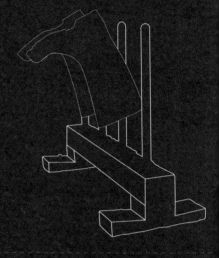

For my boot holder I recycled some old timber. You can of course use new timber, but I like the idea of creating a new and functional piece out of something that others may see as useless or unusable.

Tools & Materials

Tools:

- Drill
- Drill bit to match broom handle (or dowel) diameter
- Handsaw
- Glue
- Screws (length dependent on timber used)
- Tape measure or ruler
- Knife
- Electric sander
- Hammer (for advanced option)
- Chisel (for advanced option)

Materials:

- Dowels or broomhandles
- Timber for base (approx. 800 mm (31.49 in))
- Timber for feet pieces

Upcycling

I reused a couple of old broom handles and a roof joist for this project. The joist had a couple of notches cut out from previous joints, and also some pretty gnarly nails, but I like the character that they bring to the finished product.

Step 1:
Measure and cut base

Start by measuring out your length of timber to cut to size for the base. My holder is going to hold two sets of boots, so in order for them to not touch together, I want to leave a good amount of space between each pole.

I'm going to cut my length to 800 mm (31.49 in). This will make the first upright 100 mm (3.93 in) from one end of the length, then I'm leaving 200 mm (7.87 in) between each upright, before going back to 100 mm (3.93 in) in at the other end.

At this stage, if you're using a longer piece of wood, be sure to keep the offcuts for later — you can use them for your feet.

Step 2: Measure and mark base

Lay your tape measure or ruler on your cut length and make your marks for drilling. Like I mentioned in the step above: be sure to leave plenty of space between each mark so your boots won't knock together.

While you're making these measurements, you can also measure the width of your wood and mark the middle points too, to be sure the holes are nice and centred.

Step 3: Measure boots

Put your ruler or tape measure inside the boot to measure how long you'll want to cut your poles to. I'd say about 400 mm (15.74 in) should do the trick for most boots and shoes.

With this step it's good to add another 40 mm (1.57") onto the final size you're going to cut to. This is because you'll be drilling holes for your pole to go into the base, so if you drill 40 mm (1.57 in) deep, then you'll still have the 400 mm (15.74 in) length to fit your boots.

Step 4:
Measure, mark and cut uprights

Mark out the length on your poles (or whatever else you're using) and cut to length. Once you've cut the wood to the length you want, grab your ruler or tape measure and measure the diameter of your pole.

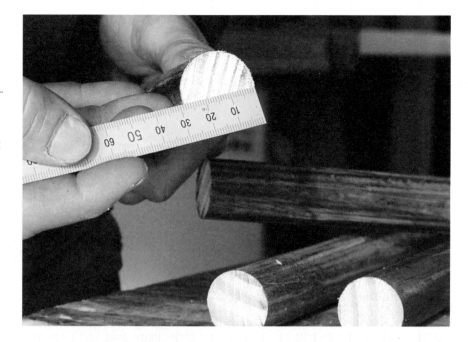

Step 5:
Drill base

Find a drill bit to match the diameter of your pole. Measure the depth you want to drill and put a piece of masking tape around your drill bit as a guide.

As mentioned in a previous step, I'm drilling around 40 mm (1.57 in) deep into my base, and using my pillar drill to ensure the holes are nice and straight.

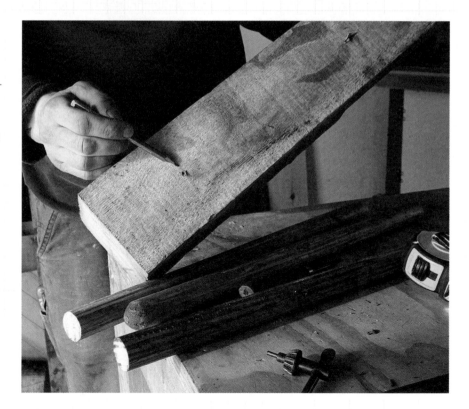

Step 6:
Drill pilot holes

Next we make pilot holes for your screws to go through, and into your upright lengths. The initial holes ensure the wood doesn't split when screwing.

Take a smaller drill bit, about 4–5mm (0.15–0.19 in), and drill through your large hole until the drill bit appears out the bottom of your base.

If your drill bit is smaller than your uprights …

whittle a little width off the bottom of the poles using a knife. It's a nice and easy job, and cheaper than heading out to buy a specific size of drill bit. Just be sure to make the knife cuts at the same height, so they're not seen when the poles are pushed into the holes.

Step 7: Shape poles

In order for your poles to look consistent, take a knife or file and round off the top of the cut ends to shape them. Then give them a quick sand with some rough sandpaper to soften any knife marks. This step is purely for aesthetics, so that the uprights look smoother.

Step 8: Sand

Take your electric sander and give all or your pieces a good sand down to clean them off, or sand by hand. I'm going to use a fairly coarse paper (80 grit).

Be sure to sand down the offcuts or extra wood you'll be using for feet too.

Advanced option:
Shaping feet

My feet pieces each already had a cut-out on one side from an old half-lap roof joint, so I recreated that on the other side of each to match. If you want to cut the timber of your feet down a bit for a similar look, you can follow these steps too.

A:
Measure and mark

Grab your two feet pieces and place your piece of base timber on top of them, so the sides of all the pieces sit flush.

Draw a line down the edge of the base piece onto the feet. If you have a cut-out like mine, measure down to this, and mark the same depth all the way around on the side you're going to cut.

If you have a plain bit of wood and need to cut both sides, place your base timber on top of your two feet pieces, making sure it's centred. Measure down to your preferred depth for your cut-out, and repeat on the other side.

B: Cut

Using a handsaw, cut a horizontal line across each foot to the depth you've marked out.

C: Chisel

Clamp your wood to your bench. With a hammer and chisel, begin to chisel away the unwanted wood, starting on the end grain and chiselling towards your cut. Be careful not to take too much off at a time and keep the chisel nice and flat.

D: Finish

When you feel you've taken a lot of waste wood away and you're close to your line, put the hammer aside. Then just use strength to carefully push the chisel, for a more accurate finish. Keep the back of the chisel nice and flat on the wood. There are plenty of videos and tutorials online to help with your chiselling technique. If you started with a plain piece of timber, repeat this step on the other side.

Step 9: Glue

If you're happy with how the feet are looking, then it's time to start gluing.

Put a drop of glue into the holes and spread some around the bottom of your uprights.

Applying some pressure, push the poles into the holes. If they're a little stiff, you can put a block of wood on the top of the poles and tap them with a hammer. This block of wood will prevent the hammer damaging the top of the poles.

Step 10: Screw poles

Turn the whole project onto its side and through the hole you drilled earlier, screw your screws into your poles to secure them in place.

Be sure to keep the poles nice and straight.

Step 11: Glue and screw feet

Glue the feet in place on the bottom of your holder, then clamp them. Drill pilot holes into the feet first, then drill your screws through. Take your clamps off.

Step 12: Display

Spin your boot holder the right way up, then go ahead and start using it!

Variations:

In the past I've made these in all sorts of different shapes and sizes, to accommodate more pairs of boots or even children's boots.

Try cutting your poles to shorter lengths and putting them alongside larg-er lengths. You can even make a holder with two rows, to put children's boots along the front row and adult boots along the back row.

Project
06.
Wooden scoop

For this project I used a piece of apple wood. I've worked with a friend doing tree surgery for a few years, and this is a piece from a beautiful old apple tree we cut down 20 minutes from my workshop. This is still fairly green, so it'll be nice and easy to work with.

Tools & Materials

Tools:

- Ruler
- Pair of compasses
- Carving knife (I use a Mora 106 carving knife)
- Wood carving gouge or crook knife (spoon knife)
- Jigsaw or bandsaw

Materials:

- I'd recommend using a piece of "green" timber. "Green" wood is the term used for wood that has recently been cut, so still has a lot of internal moisture, which makes it easier to work with. You can still carve with seasoned (dry) wood, but just be aware that it'll be a little harder to work with.

Step 1: Measure and mark

Taking your piece of timber and a ruler, draw a line down the centre of your piece of wood.

Step 2:
Draw circles

Pick up your compasses and pop the point on your centre line, ready to draw two circles – one for the bowl of your spoon and one for the edge of the bowl.

Be sure to leave a healthy gap between the second circle and the edge of your wood. This gives you a little space to work with, and for mistakes in case you gouge or knife slips while carving.

Step 3:
Draw handle

Take a ruler and draw the handle from the bowl of your spoon down the length of your wood.

Draw a neck tapering from the bowl to the handle, rather than just have your handle go straight up to the bowl. This will make carving a little easier later on.

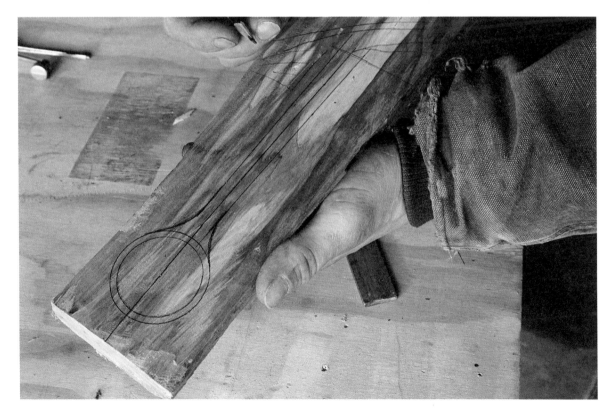

Step 4: Carve and sand bowl

Now, either clamp your wood down to your work bench, or do what I did and screw a block of scrap wood either side of your carving wood to hold it in place. (This second method gave me a little more space to work, without having to manoeuvre around clamps poking up from the bench.)

Use your gouge or crook knife to start carving out the bowl of your spoon.

Once the bowl is carved out, take a bit of 120-grit sandpaper and give the bowl of your spoon a sand. This will just take away any imperfections of marks left by your gouge or knife.

Carving tools ...

I use both a crook knife and a gouge, so it's just down to you on what's more comfortable and natural. I picked up this gouge from a local flea market. They're often the best places to find great woodworking tools for a low price, so after a quick clean up and sharpen, this is my tool of choice when it comes to spoon carving.

Step 5: Cut

Use a jigsaw or bandsaw to carefully cut the shape of your spoon out, along the outer lines you've drawn. Now you've got what's called a "blank" for your spoon.

Small bandsaws can be picked up for a really good price nowadays, but if you can't get one then just use a jigsaw. These are a great and affordable alternative to a bandsaw.

If you're using a jigsaw, be sure to clamp down your wood tightly to your work bench and follow the safety instructions included with the jigsaw. If you're using a bandsaw, then be careful to keep your fingers out the way!

Step 6: Carve back

Start working on your spoon blank with your straight carving knife. There are plenty of different ways to hold and handle a carving knife that can be found online, but a lot of it's down to the user and, above all, just feeling comfortable with it in your hands.

Start on the back of the spoon, taking some of the weight off around the bowl. Be sure to cut just a little bit off at a time – once it's gone, it's gone!

Remember to be very aware of where your fingers are at all times while using the knife.

Tip:

The two main carving grips I use are a pull stroke to my chest and a thumb push, often used for smoothing the spoon or taking chips away from the back of the bowl. The pull stroke seems counter-intuitive and even dangerous, but at this angle your hand should always hit your body before the blade. The thumb push is self-explanatory. Holding the spoon and knife tightly in each hand, use your thumb (the one holding the spoon blank) to apply pressure and push the back of the blade.

Step 7:
Carve front

When you're happy with the shape of the back of your spoon, flip it around and start working on the front.

Throughout carving, be aware how much wood you're taking away from the handle. It's easy to get distracted and take too much off, resulting in it becoming too thin and snapping.

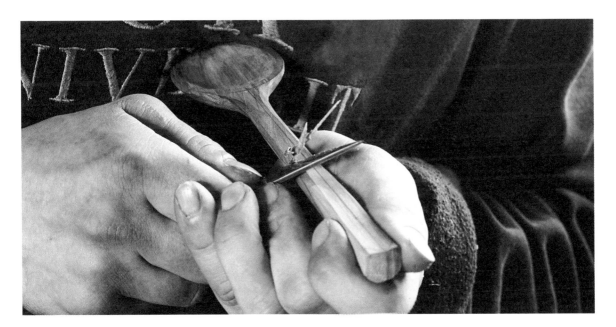

Step 8: Choose a look

When you're happy with the overall shape of your spoon, you have a couple of options to choose from.

You can either grab some sandpaper and sand the whole thing to a nice and smooth finish, or – if you're like me and want the handmade-look with the knife marks – you can leave it as it is, creating a bit more of a story to the piece.

Step 9: Oil

Once you've decided how to leave your spoon, you can put your finish on. This is an important step to maintaining the life of your spoon (or any other wooden utensil or chopping board). By adding this finish you're adding a little moisture protection which will help keep your spoon looking fresh for as long as possible. If you're just going to have the spoon as a decorative piece then I'd still suggest putting a finish on it as it brings out the grain and natural beauty of the wood.

I use a balm, or wood butter, that I've made from melting coconut oil and beeswax. Check out the resource section of this book for instructions on how to make this balm. There are loads of different finishes you can put on wooden utensils and boards, but this is something I've used since I started making wooden pieces, and it seems to work great.

Step 10: Dry and polish

Once your spoon has been oiled, leave it for a few hours to allow the balm to soak into the wood. Then use a clean, dry cloth or rag to wipe off any excess.

Project
07.
Milking stool

For this particular piece I used some locally sourced oak. A friend kindly messaged me just after a big storm that took a huge tree down opposite his house, and said he'd saved me some. For the seat part of the stool, I used my chainsaw to cut a rough block out.

Tools & Materials

Tools:

- Pair of compasses
- Plane
- Jigsaw
- Tape measure
- Chisel
- Rough file
- Pillar drill (or power drill)
- Saw

Materials:

- A piece of timber 30–40 mm (1.18–1.57 in) thick and no smaller than 200 x 200 mm (7.87 in x 7.87 in) wide. Try contacting your local timber yard when it comes to sourcing your wood. They'll often have offcuts they'd be happy to get rid of and can easily cut wood to your specifications.
- Three wood lengths 25 x 25 mm (1 x 1 in) and at least 340 mm (13.3 in) long. This will be long enough to cut off 40 mm (1.57 in) to use for the wedges.

Step 1:
Mark the seat

Using your compasses, find a rough centre point in your wood and mark a circle.

↙

Advanced option:

It's worth sticking to the guidelines here to start off, but in the future when you feel a little more confident, I'd encourage you to try different shapes and sizes for this stool. The skills you'll learn are really easily transferable to a larger scale, so why not give it a go with a rectangular top and longer, thicker legs, and try to make a bigger stool or bench for sitting on.

Step 2: Cut

Now, using your jigsaw, cut out your circle shape. Be sure to hold both the saw and the wood nice and tight when you're cutting.

(My piece of wood is pretty thick, so its maxed out the length of my jigsaw blade. That's why I'd advise using timber only 30–40 mm (1.18–1.57 in) thick.)

Step 3: Plane

When you're happy with the shape, take your smoothing plane and plane the piece of wood flat. This step is only really necessary if you've had to cut the wood yourself, or if your wood is particularly rough or uneven.

The purpose of a plane is to flatten a surface and leave it smoother than it was before. No.4 planes are super common and can be found nice and cheaply in a tool shop, or even cheaper at car boot sales.

Step 4: Mark the legs

Draw a line about 35 mm (1.37 in) in from the edge of the timber. Then make three evenly spaced pencil marks on your circular pencil line. You can use the compasses for this, to make the distances a little more equal than if you just do it by eye.

Step 5: Taper and cut legs

Now get your leg lengths and clamp them nice and tightly to your bench. You could also put them in a vice to keep them secure while shaping.

I like the look of the legs being a little tapered towards the top, so I'm going to use my plane to shave some of the wood off and shape the legs a little.

Once you're happy with the taper, cut your legs to size.

Step 6: Drill

Set the table on the pillar drill to an angle of 10 degrees, so you'll set the legs at a slight slant for a more traditional look.

Find a drill bit that's a similar size to the tapered end of your legs. Drill a hole right through your seat timber at each point where you made a pencil mark.

I use my pillar drill for accuracy – you can use a hand drill if you're careful, but I've found it's a lot easier to get the angle spot on if you're using a pillar drill.

Step 7:
Fit legs

Once the holes are drilled, take a carving knife or Stanley knife and neaten the tapered ends of your legs.

Try your best to make them a more circular shape to fit neatly into the holes. But don't worry about not getting them perfectly round, as long as they fit snugly in your drilled holes.

Step 8: Test and number

It's good practice to test fit as often as possible with these sorts of projects. It's the best way to ensure that everything fits and looks good before you commit to gluing things permanently.

When you're happy with the fit, flip the stool upside down and put a number on the bottom of each leg, and the same number next to each leg's corresponding hole. This means you'll be able to get the legs to match when you come to gluing.

Step 9:
Cut slots

When you've tested the rough fit and numbered the legs, take your stool apart again and put the seat aside.

Clamp the legs to your workbench, or use a vice to secure the legs upright, then take your saw and cut little slots in the top of the legs. These are going to be used to create a wedged tenon joint to secure your legs in place later on.

Be careful to not cut too far down – use the thickness of the seat as a gauge to how far you should go, and try not to go any deeper.

Step 10: Make wedges

When it comes to making the wedges to secure the legs in their holes, just grab some offcuts. Some people like to use a contrasting timber to the one they're using for the legs, but that's totally up to you or whatever you have in your workshop. I used some oak I had knocking about.

This joint works by forcing the tenon apart when the wedge is driven into it. On this occasion, the tenon is the tapered end of the leg that goes into the seat. By hammering the wedge into the slot you cut, it forces each side of the leg apart, holding the leg firmly in place.

To help me make the wedges, I screwed a scrap of timber about the width of the top end of the stool legs onto my workbench. Then I could put my offcut up to the screwed-down scrap and push my chisel into it, taking shavings off until the offcut was a suitable wedge shape.

Step 11:
Shape and smooth

I didn't want the edges of my stool to be too harsh, so clamped the seat to my workbench and used a chisel to take some material off the edges.

I used my original inner circular pencil mark as a guide for where to chisel, to make sure the same amount was taken off the whole way around. I then used a rasp file to soften the edges and make the chisel marks.

I used my orbital sander for a nice, smooth finish, starting at around 80 grit to take off the worst marks, then up to 120 and even 180 to ensure the stool was very smooth.

Step 12: Glue

Pop some glue on the top of the legs and push each leg through the hole with its corresponding number.

Remember to add a little bit of glue into the wedge slots, then carefully hammer your wedges into the slots until they all fit tightly. As you hammer the wedges you'll see the tenon forced apart, securing the legs in their holes. Don't overdo it as you run the risk of splitting your seat.

Wipe any excess glue away with a damp rag, then grab your saw and cut off the excess leg poking through the top of your seat.

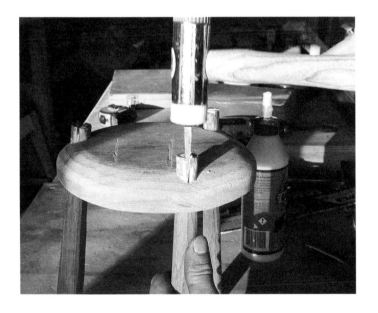

Step 13: Trim and tidy

Use a chisel around the leg holes, to trim and tidy any wood you didn't manage to cut with your saw. This will make the wedge joints nice and flush with the top of your seat.

Step 14: Level legs

To finish off, place your stool on the workbench and check it's straight. If it's not, then it's easy to spot which leg is making it unbalanced. Use a saw to take just a little bit off it at a time until the stool stands nice and flat.

Step 15: Oil

When you're happy with your stool you can give the whole thing a coat of oil. I'm using a simple Danish oil because it provides a nice hard-wearing finish and is often water resistant.

Apply with a brush or clean, dry cloth. Wait for 10 minutes, then wipe off any excess.

Project
08.
Wall-mounted tool storage

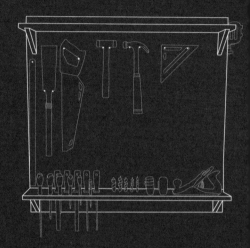

The great thing about this project is how adaptable it can be made to fit around you, your tools and your workspace. Whether you have a dedicated workshop or the corner of a room, this storage unit can be built to fit.

Tools & Materials

Tools:

- Tape measure
- Screws
- Drill
- Saw
- Various drill bits for holes on shelf
- Plane
- Blow torch or black paint
- Brass frame mounting plates
- 45 mm (1.77 in) nails

Materials:

- Approx 8 m (26 ft) of pine, 170 mm x 20 mm
  (6.69 in x 0.78 in)
- 2 x 1 m (3.3 ft) lengths of pine, 20 mm x 45 mm
  (0.78 in x 1.77in)

Step 1:
Measure and cut wood

Start by cutting your 170 mm x 20 mm (6.69 in x 0.78 in) pine to make boards 1 m (3.3 ft) long. You'll need six to make your storage board 1 m (3.3 ft) wide. (Keep the remaining 2 m (6.6 ft) of pine for the shelves in Step 4.)

Lay the six boards out on your work bench and measure their total width. Cut a piece of 20 mm x 45 mm (0.78 in x 1.77 in) pine to match this measurement.

Step 2:
Plane edges

Put aside the two pieces you just cut and grab your hand plane. Holding it at a 45-degree angle, pass it along the edges of the boards to soften them. You could do this step with a piece of sandpaper too. This isn't a crucial step, but I'm doing it for the aesthetic.

Step 3: Screw battens

Put your board timbers face down on your bench and lay your 20 mm x 45 mm (0.78 in x 1.77 in) battens along the top and bottom. Make sure they're equally spaced all the way along, then clamp and screw them onto the boards to hold everything together.

Step 4: Cut shelves and brackets

Flip the whole thing over and measure the width again. Cut two pieces of 170 mm x 20 mm (6.69 in x 0.78 in) pine as shelves. Make corner brackets from offcuts or any leftover timber by marking a 160 mm x 160 mm (6.29 in x 6.29 in) square, drawing a diagonal from one edge to the other and cutting the lines with a hand saw. Repeat the step for another set of brackets for the other shelf.

Step 5:
Sand and check brackets

Give the shelf brackets a good sand down and test them to check they fit with the shelves.

Optional detailing:

This step is purely for aesthetics. You can do anything from paint your back board, to varnish it, or even just leave it as it is. The decision is totally yours.

One great option is to put the shelves, brackets and any tools aside and grab your blowtorch. Set the blowtorch to a medium flame and begin passing it over your boards. The idea is to scorch the wood and lightly darken it, not burn it. Follow up with a light sanding over the scorched wood to remove any frayed fibres.

Be really careful when using a blowtorch, and keep any loose clothes and tools out of the way. Always follow the manufacturer's instructions.

Step 6:
Screw on top shelf brackets

Mark on the board where your top brackets need to go. I set mine in from the edge by about 25 mm (0.98 in), and approximately 80 mm (3.14 in) from the top. Drill a hole through the front of the board first, then cover the hole with your bracket and drill in through the back. This will make the last part – screwing in the screws – easier. Repeat for the second top bracket.

Step 7:
Screw on top shelf

Screw your top shelf onto the brackets, then screw through the back into your shelf to ensure it's really secure.

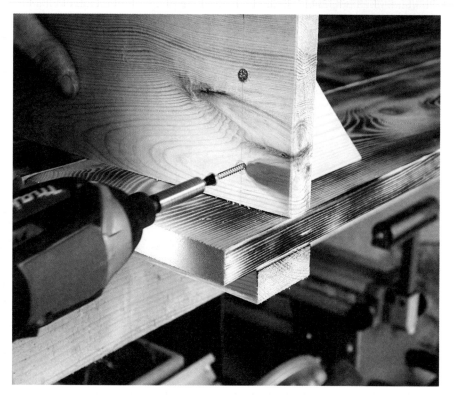

Step 8: Mark tool holes

For the bottom shelf, grab a tape measure or ruler and mark out where you want to drill the holes that will hold your tools. I opted for a few different sizes to accommodate different sized tools. I also only drilled my holes on about a third of my shelf, so there's space left to stand other tools.

Step 9: Drill tool holes

Drill your holes, being sure to flip your wood over and drill from underneath first, before drilling all the way through from the top. This will prevent the grain blowing out. Keeping the bottom of the brackets flush with the bottom line of the back board, repeat Steps 6 and 7 to affix your bottom shelf to the back board.

Step 10:
Screw mounting plates

Screw your two brass frame mounting plates onto the top batten on the back, so your tool storage can be hung on the wall.

Step 11:
Add hanging nails

To hang your tools simply lay or hold them where you want them to go, and hammer nails into the back board to hang them in place.

Project
09.
Concrete planter

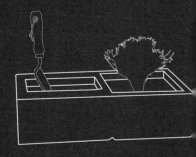

To make moulds for these planters, I used some old laminate doors. Laminate stops the moisture from the concrete mix soaking into the wood, so it's easier to remove from the mould, and they're easy to come by as they're always being thrown out. Save them from landfill with this simple project.

Tools & Materials

Tools:

- Bucket
- Sponge or rag
- Spade
- Trowel
- Drill
- Saw
- Silicone
- Screws
- Sander
- Rubber mallet or hammer
- Set square
- Ruler or tape measure

Materials:

- Bag of cement
- Bag of coarse sand (ballast)
- Old laminate kitchen units

Step 1:
Mark and cut large box

Start by marking and cutting your kitchen units to build a good-sized box. I'm making my length, width and height 500 mm x 300 mm x 150 mm (19.6 in x 11.8 in x 5.9 in). Before cutting, use a sharp knife to score a line on the laminate – this will prevent the laminate splitting too much when cutting.

Step 2:
Check and screw large box

When you've cut your pieces, hold the box together to make sure it all fits okay, then begin screwing it together. It's important to drill pilot holes before screwing, this time to prevent the chip board splitting when you screw in the screws.

Step 3: Seal large box

Now we'll use silicone to seal any gaps inside the box, so there are no leaks of moisture and so the edges of the concrete are nice and smooth when you take your planter out of the mould. Silicone is really easy to use. Just place your box on the workbench, then squeeze a bead around all the inside joins of the box where the sides meet. Then run a wet finger over the bead to smooth it off. After a couple of moments, grab a damp sponge and wipe over all the joins again to clean up any excess silicone.

Step 4: Measure and cut small boxes

Measure the inside of your large box and cut your remaining lengths of laminate to make two small boxes that are at least 25 mm (1 in) shallower in length, width and height. This will allow plenty of space for the concrete.

The three boxes together will make a negative mould for us to pour the concrete into. The planter I'm making has two spaces, but if you want more or less, then make mould boxes accordingly.

Remember: The more complicated the planter, the trickier it'll be to remove from the mould.

Step 5:
Seal smaller boxes

When you've made your smaller boxes grab your silicone again, but instead of squeezing it on the inside, put a bead around the cuts on the outsides these boxes. This should help seal the chipboard a little bit and stop it soaking up moisture. Use your finger to spread the silicone along the cut, then again give it a wipe with a damp sponge to clean it up.

Step 6:
Outline and drill

Place your first smaller box inside the larger box where you want it to be fixed. Using a ruler or tape measure, ensure that it's evenly spaced and perfectly square. Draw around it with a pencil to transfer the shape onto the base of your large box.

When you remove the smaller box, you'll see the outline of it in the large box. Drill holes just inside the pencil marks – these will indicate where to screw the screws that will secure the small box inside the large box to stop it floating out of place when we pour the concrete mix in.

Repeat for the second smaller box.

Step 7: Secure boxes

Carefully hold the first of your smaller boxes in place and drill your screws through the base of the large box and into the smaller box to secure it in place. Be really careful to make sure your boxes are lined up with the pencil marks you made in Step 6.

Repeat for the second smaller box.

Step 8: Mix and pour concrete

When you're happy with your mould you can start making up the concrete mix. Grab your bucket, cement and ballast. Make the mix with one spade of cement to four spades of ballast. This should create a strong final mix.

Add small amounts of water at a time and thoroughly mix the ballast and cement together. Be sure to get to the bottom of the bucket. Mix with a spade or trowel, then pour or spade it into your mould, being sure to cover over your small boxes with at least 25 mm (1 in) depth of the concrete mix. This will eventually become the bottom of your planter, so we want to make sure there's enough mixture to become the base.

Step 9: Settle concrete

Use a sander without a sanding pad to vibrate the mixture. You can also use a rubber mallet to tap the sides. This step will help the mixture to settle in the bottom of the mould, and will also raise any air bubbles to the top of your mould. When you're happy with how your mould is looking with the mix inside, put it aside and leave for at least five days.

Step 10: Remove moulds

After five days, carefully take the planter out of the mould. I found the best way was to carefully deconstruct the mould and with a mixture of tapping and shaking, slide the inside boxes out of the planter. This takes great patience and care. Rushing this step could result in cracking and breaking your planter.

Step 11: Fill planter

Finally, fill your planter with compost and plant some plants.

These are perfect for putting on the kitchen windowsill as a handy planter for various herbs. They're also great for filling with succulents for a bedroom or living room to add a great modern industrial look to any space.

Project
10.
Magnetic
knife-holder

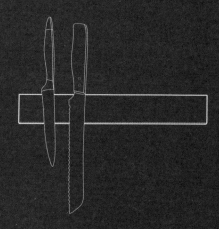

A super-minimal and neat way to hold your kitchen knives. Try using some timber with an interesting grain pattern to make it a nice piece to look at even with no knives on it.

Tools & Materials

Tools:

- Drill
- Drill bit the same diameter as magnets
- Masking tape
- Sander
- Saw
- Set square
- Chisel
- 8 mm (0.31 in) plug cutter or dowel
- 8 mm (0.31 in) drill bit to match size of plug cutter or dowel
- Ruler or tape measure
- Spirit level

Materials:

- Length of hardwood (oak, beech, walnut are good choices) approx. 25 mm x 45 mm x 350 mm (0.78 in x 1.77 in x 13.77 in).
- Small, strong magnets

Step 1:
Measure and cut wood

Begin by selecting your piece of wood. I'm using a nice piece of beech which has a unique grain.

Measure and mark your piece to a suitable length – around 300 mm or 320 mm (11.8 in or 12.5 in) is a good size, as this will then leave you a little bit of off-cut to make some plugs later.

To cut the piece neatly, score the pencil line with a sharp knife. Then, coming from the waste side of the wood, carefully push your chisel up to the knife mark to create a channel. Your saw will sit in here nicely and ensure an accurate cut. After you've cut, use a sharp chisel to pare the end grain and clean it up.

Step 2:
Drill screw holes

Measure and mark where you want to drill your holes to screw the knife holder onto the wall. Around 20 mm (0.8 in) in from the end, and nice and in the middle of your piece of wood is a good place to drill the hole.

Take your 8 mm (0.3 in) drill bit and drill into the timber. You'll only need to drill around 5 mm (0.19 in) deep, then swap the drill bit for a smaller one and drill a pilot hole for the screw.

Step 3:
Measure and mark magnet holes

Flip your wood over so it's face down and measure out lines across it, spaced at equal distances, from one end to the other. This is going to be the distance between your magnets. I marked my lines out at 30 mm (1.2 in) apart.

Now make three marks on each line – again you want to ensure they're equally spaced. I made marks 10 mm (0.39 in) in from each side, then at 22 mm (0.86 in) for down the middle.

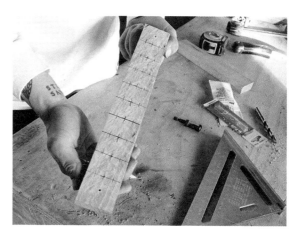

Step 4: Drill magnet holes

You'll want to drill holes for the magnets that go close as you can to the other side without going through. Measure the drilling depth and mark this with a piece of masking tape on the drill bit that's the same diameter as your magnets.

Drill your holes on each pencil mark you've made in the previous steps. It's definitely best to use a pillar drill for this step to ensure absolute accuracy, but it can be done very carefully with a normal cordless (or corded) drill.

Step 5: Sand

When you've drilled all your holes, give the back a good pass over with your sander, just to clean out the tops of the holes you've drilled and neaten them up.

Step 6: Insert magnets

Lay your magnets alongside your wood to see how many you'll need for each hole, then hammer them into the holes. Be careful not to hit them too hard or you might ruin the main face of the knife holder.

Step 7:
Cut plugs

Grab an offcut of your timber and, using the 8 mm (0.31 in) plug cutter in your drill, drill into the wood and cut out plugs. An alternative would be just to buy some 8 mm (0.31 in) dowels, but for this project I prefer to use the exact same wood for the plugs as the rest of the knife holder.

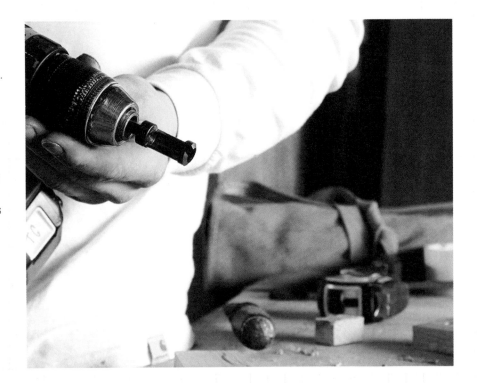

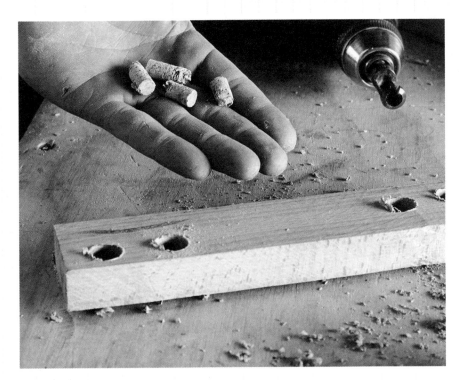

Step 8: Oil wood

Sand your knife holder down and give it a coat of good waterproof oil. This will not only help to protect your knife holder, but it'll also make the grain pop to create a truly unique piece for your home.

Step 9: Screw onto wall

Screw your knife holder to the wall, using a spirit level.

Step 10:
Fill plug holes

Add a drop of glue in the plug holes and push the plugs or dowels in. If they're a little tight just give them a tap with a hammer. If any parts of the plugs poke out, you can neaten them by grabbing a sharp chisel and shaving off any excess.

Dab a little oil on your plugs so they match the rest of the wood, and then the project should be complete.

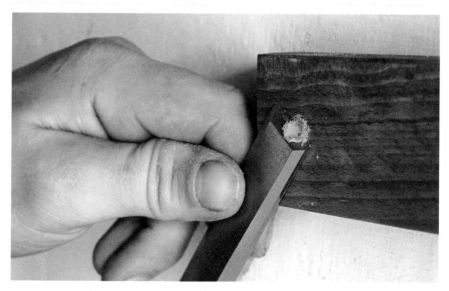

Project
11.
Weaving loom

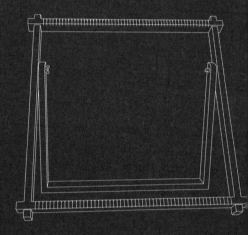

I began making weaving looms as special commissions for a friend in London but they quickly became one of my most asked-about and sold products. It's been great to contribute to the evolution of the ancient craft of weaving into a more modern and recognized art.

Tools & Materials

Tools:

- Band saw or jigsaw
- Ruler or tape measure
- Chisel
- Set square
- Glue
- Sander
- 8 mm (0.31 in) dowel
- 8 mm (0.31in) drill bit
- Drill
- Wing nuts and bolts
- Drill bit to match diameter of bolts

Materials:

- 7 m (23 ft) of oak 20 mm x 45 mm x (0.78 in x 1.77 in)

Step 1:
Cut oak

Measure, mark and cut four
lengths of oak to 600 mm
(23.6 in).

Step 2:
Measure and
mark joints

Now we're going to make half lap
joints to make strong corners for
the loom. Take your first cut length
and make a mark 20 mm (0.78 in)
down from the end and 40 mm
(1.57 in) in from the edge.

Using your set square, draw a
line at each mark at 90 degrees
to each other. Measure 20 mm
(0.78 in) down the side of the
timber as a depth mark. Do this
on both ends of all four lengths.

Step 3: Cut and chisel joints

Clamp your timber against the side of your bench or put it in a vice and, using your saw, cut down to your 20 mm (0.78 in) depth. Now use a chisel to remove the waste wood and clean your cut out.

Step 4: Check fit

When you've cut and chiselled the joints, push everything together to check it all fits okay. When taking the loom apart after test-fitting, mark numbers inside the joint cuts so you know to match the corresponding numbers up again next time you fit it together.

Step 5:
Mark notches

Decide which lengths you'd like to use as the top and bottom of your loom, ready to make notches in them for your yarn. Lay the lengths on the bench and mark 45 mm (1.77 in) in from the end, then mark every 10 mm (0.39 in) along and at 10 mm (0.39in) deep. If you hold both lengths together, you can draw the lines at the same time to save a bit of time (as pictured).

Tip:

Band saws are another great, fairly inexpensive tool to have around the workshop. You can pick up pretty basic ones brand new for a good price, and used ones even cheaper. The one I'm using for this project was actually given to me, showing how readily available they are.

Step 6:
Cut notches

With a jigsaw or band saw, start cutting each line. If you're using a jigsaw make sure you clamp the wood tightly on your work bench and hold the jigsaw tightly so it doesn't bounce around.

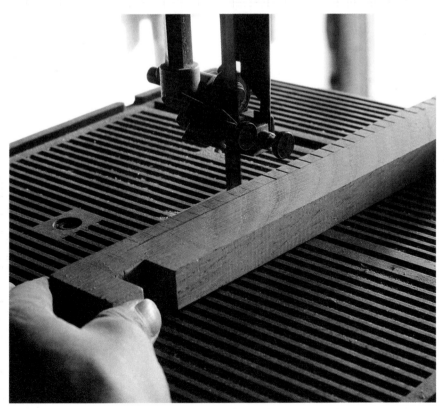

Step 7:
Secure joints

When you've made the notch cuts, give the lengths of oak a sand down. Then put a dab of glue in each joint and push your timbers together.

If necessary, give the joints a little tap with a hammer to secure them. Always protect your timber by putting a block of wood between it and your hammer, rather than hammering directly onto your project.

At this point your loom will be good to use but follow the next steps to learn how to make a fold-out stand for it.

Step 8: Cut lengths

Take your remaining oak and cut two lengths to 400 mm (15.78 in).

Now lay the two cut pieces on either side of the inside of your loom, and measure the distance between them. Cut another length of oak to fit this gap.

Tip

There are dozens of instructional weaving and tapestry videos to be found online – it's easy to get your loom set up and create a simple table mat or wall hanging. Use strips of cloth from old clothes for a truly individual and ethical piece.

Step 9:
Screw stand

Clamp your three stand pieces together, or lay them flat on your bench, and screw them together to make an inner frame shape. As in other projects, drill 8 mm (0.31 in) pilot holes to start, then screw into those and cover the screw ends with dowel. (There's more about how to do this in Step 9 of the bookshelf project on p124.)

Step 10:
Check stand fit

Place the stand inside the loom. Make sure it's about 10 mm (0.39 in) up from the bottom of the loom to allow for the stand to swing out.

Step 11:
Measure and mark bolt holes

Measure and mark on the stand where you're going to drill through either side to fit the bolts. Ensure everything is really even and straight, then drill through both the stand and the loom with your drill bit to match the bolts you'll be using.

Step 12: Chisel corner

Put the bolts through the holes and open the stand out away from the loom. Make a pencil mark on the small corner that pokes out at the front of the loom. Take the stand and loom apart again, and using a sharp chisel, pare off the corner. Smooth it off either by hand with the chisel or with a sander.

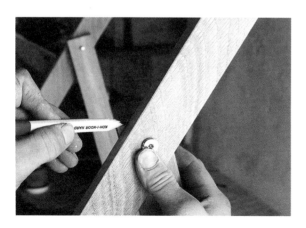

Step 13:
Sand and finish

Sand the loom and the frame
down. I wouldn't usually oil the
weaving looms but the grain
on this oak was too nice, so I
wanted to oil it to make the grain
pop. I used simple Danish oil
for this.

Step 14:
Assemble

Put your loom together and give
the wing nuts a tighten by hand.
When you want to use the loom,
simply loosen the wing nuts and
pull your stand out, then tighten
the nuts up again.

Project

12.

Coffee table

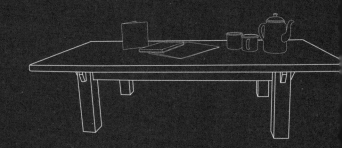

We'll make this table using a castle joint
– the tops of the legs will be cut and end
up looking like turrets on a castle. We'll
also create half-lap joints to sit in between
the turrets, making a solid table that can
cope with weight and pressure.

Tools & Materials

Tools:

- Drill
- Hand saw
- Tape measure or ruler
- Screw driver
- Screw
- Set square
- Chisel
- Hammer
- Glue
- Sander

Materials:

- Small corner brackets
- The length and width of the timber you need depends on the size of the table you're making. You could use one solid piece for the top, or even two separate pieces with a join down the middle.

  As a guide:
  65 mm x 65 mm (2.55 in x 2.55 in) for the legs
  20 mm x 45 mm (0.78 in x 1.77 in) for the top frame
  25 mm (0.98 in) thick wood for the table top

Step 1: Cut legs

Begin by marking and cutting the 65 mm x 65 mm (2.55 in x 2.55 in) leg pieces to length. I'm just using a handsaw to cut these to around 250 mm (9.84 in), but you can cut yours to a height that suits you.

Step 2:
Measure and mark castle joints

Mark the centre point of your legs with a cross, then measure and mark 10 mm (0.39 in) either side of each line to create a cross shape 20 mm (0.78 in) wide from three lines.

Now, using a set square, draw lines down the length of each side to a depth of 45 mm (1.77 in). You'll cut to this depth mark in the next step.

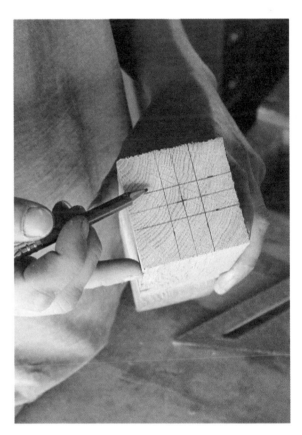

Step 3: Cut castle joints

Clamp the leg upright and, from the top, cut down the lines until you reach your depth marks. This is called a "rip cut" which is when you cut parallel to the grain.

I start the cut with my standard handsaw, then continue the cut with my vintage rip saw. There's no real benefit to using the vintage saw other than the pleasure of using old tools. I have however found that this particular rip saw does cut a lot faster and cleaner than my newer saw, which is a real testament to some of the older kit you can pick up these days.

Step 4: Chisel castle joints

Now clamp the piece horizontally onto the bench and use a chisel to start taking out the bulk of the waste wood between your cuts.

Start at the depth mark and work your way up toward the end of the leg, then change direction, chiselling from the end grain back towards the pencil mark. This is a pretty simple and effective way of chiselling waste wood out. Repeat until you've removed all the waste.

Step 5: Pare joints

To clean up the joint after removing the waste, use a nice, sharp chisel to pare across the grain inside. This is also the best technique to use to adjust the fit of your joint if you find it's too tight.

Step 6:
Mark and cut top frame

Decide how long and wide you want your table to be and cut your 20 mm x 45 mm (0.78 in x 1.77 in) lengths to the right size.

Lay your cut lengths on your bench and place the leg upside down (that is, joint side down). Draw in pencil around the joint shape to transfer the inside and outside edges of the joint onto the timber lengths.

Step 7:
Measure and mark half-lap joints

Now we'll create what's called a "half-lap joint", which involves removing half the depth of wood from two pieces of wood at the point where they meet, to create a neat join.

Measure and mark the halfway point of width of your length pieces to create a depth mark for your cuts. Do the same with your width pieces. Because I like the finished look, I'm leaving a 20 mm (0.78 in) overlap on each side of the leg, rather than my wood being flush with the edges of the legs.

As you can see in the photo, the wood up to the first line will be the overhang, then up the second line is where the wood from the leg will sit, and beyond that is where the joint will be. I'll cut half the depth out of each piece of 20 mm x 45 mm (0.78 in x 1.77 in) so they to lap over each other when they're pushed together.

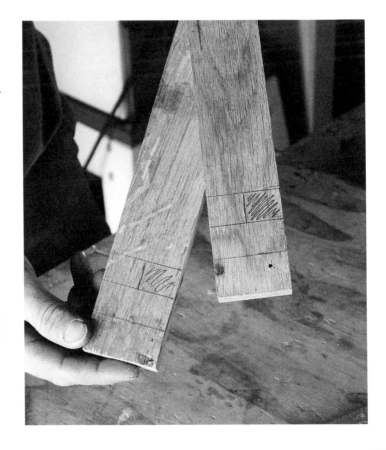

Step 8: Cut and chisel half-lap joints

On each piece of wood cut down the lines to depth marks. Chisel the waste away as we did in Steps 4 and 5, then give it a test fit. It should be nice and tight, but it's not critical if it isn't — the whole thing will be held snug in the main castle joint on the leg. This is where you see the joint really come together.

Step 9: Test fit and sand

Once you've repeated the steps above for all of the legs and joints, test fit the whole thing – legs and frame pieces – to make sure they are nice and tight all round.

Now take it apart and give it all a good clean up with the sander. I'm using reclaimed wood so sanding is necessary, but if you've bought your timber new from a timber yard, then you could get away with skipping the sanding.

Optional detailing:

You can see I cut a little angle on the overhang part of each end of the frame pieces. I just thought it'd be a nice touch to go towards the overall aesthetic of the finished product, but it's not a necessary step.

Step 10: Screw legs and frame

Put everything back together and drill a pilot hole through the top of each joint for your screw to go through. Take it all apart again and glue the inside of the castle joint and also each half-lap joint, then put the glued pieces back together and screw through your pilot holes to fully secure your joint.

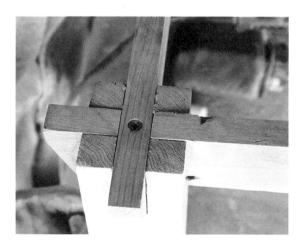

Step 11:
Fit corner brackets

Now take a handful of small corner brackets, which will help strengthen your table top. Space them out evenly and mark out on the table frame where you want them to go. I'm adding three along the longest side of the table, then four on the shorter sides. I'm using two separate pieces of timber for my table top, so this should be an ample amount of fixings to secure it in place.

To fit corner brackets, start by holding the bracket in place so the top of it is flush with the top of the table frame. Then make a pencil mark and drill a small pilot hole there, being careful not to drill all the way through the frame. Lastly screw the bracket in place.

Step 12:
Fit table top

Lay your table top upside down, then place your table frame on top of it, also upside down. Measure all the way around and make sure there's an even overhang on each side, then screw through the corner brackets into your table top, ensuring the screws are nice and tight before flipping everything over.

Step 13: Finish

It's your choice if you want to give the whole thing a coat of oil, or even just the top. I decided to leave mine natural, so it would show more obvious signs of age as it gets used more.

Project
13.
Bookshelf

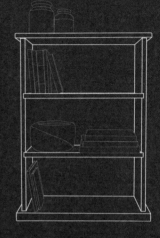

This particular piece was measured and made to fit in a specific space, but you can use the following techniques to make both larger and smaller bookshelves.

Tools & Materials

Tools:

- Saw
- Set square
- Chisel
- Ruler or tape measure
- Drill
- Hand plane
- Masking tape
- Danish oil
- 8 mm (0.31 in) drill bit
- 3mm (0.11) drill bit

Materials:

- Wood (oak)
- 5 m of 275 mm x 25 mm
  (16.4 ft of 11 in x 1 in)
- 1 m of 300 mm x 25 mm
  (3.3 ft of 12 in x 1 in)
- 1.5 m of 25 mm x 50 mm
  (5 ft of 1 in x 2 in)
- 8 mm (0.31 in) dowel
- 45 mm (1.77 in) screws

Step 1: Mark and cut

Mark out and cut two 1 m (3.3 ft) lengths to use as the upright pieces on your unit. I used my chop saw for accuracy and a nice neat cut, but this can be done by hand or even by the timber yard when you're buying your wood. It's always good to make the most of the resources timber yards and DIY stores have.

Tip:

Chop saws, or mitre saws, can be picked up really cheaply these days, and are a great tool to have about in the workshop. They make cutting more accurate and general working way more efficient.

Step 2:
Measure and mark shelves

Lay a tape measure or ruler along your timber and mark the intervals where you want your shelves to go. My largest books are around 290 mm (11.41 in) tall, so I'm making the gaps between each shelf 300 mm (11.8 in).

Mark the thickness of your shelves (25 mm,1 in) and, using your set square, draw out where the shelves will go. Transfer these lines onto the opposite upright piece too.

Step 3:
Score and mark joints

Now we make dado joints. These are really strong woodworking joints made by creating a channel cut across the grain of one piece of wood that a second piece slots into. It's best to take your time to make these nice and accurate, so the second piece fits nice and tight.

Start by laying your set square on the lines you just marked and score along them with a sharp knife. This knife mark should help you cut a little more accurately with the saw.

Draw a line along the edges of your scored pieces, at 10 mm (0.39 in). This is the depth you want to cut to for your dado joint. Repeat this step on both pieces, where the dado cuts are going to be made.

Step 4:
Make guide cuts

Using your handsaw, carefully cut along the line until you're at the desired depth.

Step 5: Chisel joints

Take your chisel and make small notches inside the two lines you just sawed. With the bevel of your chisel facing up, start chiselling between these notches. Once the channel is chiselled out, flip your chisel over so the bevel is down, and clean out your channel. Using the chisel bevel-edge down will prevent chiselling too deep into your wood.

When you've finished making the dado cuts on both your uprights, grab your shelf pieces and push everything together to test the fit. Make adjustments where needed, until everything fits tightly.

Optional detailing:

To add a neat finishing edge to the bottom of your shelves, first measure the width and the depth of the unit. Transfer these measurements onto your 50 mm x 25 mm (2 in x 1 in) length and cut the ends of each piece at a 45-degree angle on your measured marks. Either leave extra wood for these angled cuts when marking and cutting your timber, or cut 45 degrees on one side of the timber before laying it along your unit and pencil-marking where the second cut needs to

go. This bottom edge is effectively a kick plate for the bottom of your bookshelf to protect the front and sides from any scuffs or marks.

To make the cuts, use the chop saw set to 45 degrees, or a mitre box and hand saw to do it by hand. Put these pieces to one side ready for additional details later on.

Step 6: Mark screw holes

Carefully take everything apart and lay your two side pieces down. Draw a line in the middle of each dado cut on the outside of the uprights, then mark where you're going to drill your holes. (I made two holes about 45 mm (1.77 in) in from either edge).

Step 7: Drill screw holes

Begin by using the 8 mm (0.31 in) drill bit. Wrap masking tape around the bit at about 5 mm (0.19 in) depth, to give you an accurate guide. Drill holes at the points you marked in Step 6, stopping at the masking tape. Then change to a smaller drill bit (3 mm, 0.11 in) and drill right through the uprights into the shelves.

Step 8: Secure shelves

Glue and screw all the shelves into one upright, then repeat on the other side.

Advanced detailing:

Now, taking your bottom edging again, take a hand plane and add a chamfer before you fit it. Simply hold or clamp the timber to your bench and pass your plane at a 45-degree angle along its edge.

Screw the bottom edging to the rest of your shelves as before.

Step 9: Add dowels

For a nice, neat look, add dowels to all your screw holes. Just pop a little glue in each hole and push or lightly hammer the dowels into the holes, then cut them flush with a handsaw..

Tip:

I use a Ryobi saw to cut my dowels. This leaves a really neat cut, but a good handsaw will do the same job. If there's any of the dowel left hanging out after cutting, you can grab a sharp chisel and, keeping it nice and flat against the side, you can push it across the dowel to shave off thin amounts. This is called "paring".

Step 10:
Measure and cut top shelf

Measure the top of the bookshelf, then grab your remaining piece of timber and mark out the length to cut to. I added a little overhang either side of the top to keep the top and bottom of the unit balanced.

Step 11: Secure top shelf

Place the cut top piece where you want it to go, and mark where you need to add screws. Use the same drilling technique in Step 7 to drill holes and screw the top on. You can add dowels as you did before.

Step 12: Sand and finish

Sand down the whole unit to make sure it's smooth and snag free. I decided to give my bookshelf a coat of Danish oil to really make the grain pop. Just follow the steps on the back of the tin for the perfect finish.

Advanced option

When you feel comfortable with the techniques and process here, you could try dividing up the shelves by adding some vertical lengths of timber to create different shaped spaces for books and other bits and pieces.

Optional detailing:

You can add to the aesthetic by creating a nice bevel detail along the top. Use the same technique you did with plane to make the chamfer for the bottom edge.

Project
14.
Clothes rail

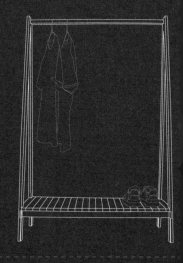

For this project, we're going to make
what are called "cross-lap" joints, a
strong join between two pieces of timber.
This involves removing half the depth
from each of the two pieces, at the point
at which they meet. These pieces then
slot together and create a flush joint.

Tools & Materials

Tools:

- Saw
- Drill
- 8 mm (0.31 in) drill bit
- Clamps
- Glue
- Chisel
- Straight edge
- Hammer
- Set square
- Ruler or tape measure

Materials:

- 1 m (3.3 ft) of 20 mm x 30 mm (0.78 in x 1.18 in) oak
- 20 m (65 ft) of 20 mm x 45 mm (0.78 in x 1.77 in) oak
- 8 mm (0.31 in) dowel
- 40 mm (1.57 in) nails with small heads

Step 1: Measure and mark joints

Start by cutting four 1.5 m (4 ft 9.2 in) lengths from your 20 x 45 mm (0.78 x 1.77 in) oak – these will make your legs – and two lengths at approximately 400 mm (15.74 in) – these will form the horizontal support between the legs. The two shorter lengths will be cut to a more specific size later. Lay two of your leg lengths on the work bench, ensuring their top ends touch. Position the bottom ends 400 mm (15.7 in) apart, while still touching at the top ends, to create an angle.

Mark 200 mm (7.87 in) up from the bottom of each leg length, and lay your first 400 mm (15.74 in) support piece across the marks. You need to mark the angles that the legs make on this piece, so you can cut it to fit. Hold your pencil underneath the piece of wood and draw a line that follows the angle of the outside edge of each leg, onto the underside of the piece of support wood. Cut along these lines and lay your timber back where it was on the pencil marks.

Step 2:
Measure, mark and chisel leg

Now draw around the outline of your support piece onto your legs and measure 10 mm (0.39 in) down on the side of the leg timbers as depth stop-marks – you shouldn't cut any deeper than this.

Using a hand saw, cut along the pencil outlines. You need to chisel out the wood within, so add some extra cuts to make it easier to chisel out the waste.

Step 3:
Measure and mark cross piece

Once you've chiselled out the waste wood from the leg parts of the joint, you need to create a matching notch on the support timber. Measure and mark 45 mm (1.75 in) from one end of this support piece and down to a depth of 10 mm (0.39 in).

Step 4:
Chisel cross piece

Cut along these lines and chisel away the waste wood again. Be careful not to go lower than your 10 mm (0.39 in) depth mark, otherwise the joint will be untidy and uneven. Always take small shavings off at a time when you're chiselling. If the joint is a little proud you can carefully just shave a little extra off one of both sides until it sits flush.

Step 5:
Glue lap joints

Glue and clamp your cross lap joint together, making sure everything is nice and tight. Repeat all the steps above for the other side.

Step 6: Cut top piece

Squeeze together the tops of the legs in their angled position and draw a straight line across them. Lay a small length of your oak along the top ends of the legs and, with a straight edge tool, mark pencil lines that carry the angles from the uprights onto the top piece. Cut along the lines on your legs and on the top piece, then test to make sure they all fit together nicely.

Step 7: Screw top piece

Add a dab of glue on the top of your legs, and clamp all three pieces to your workbench. Take your 8 mm (0.31 in) drill bit and mark it at 5 mm (0.2 in) with masking tape, so you won't drill any deeper than this. Drill guide holes into the top piece toward the legs, to the depth of the tape. Insert your screws into these guide holes and join the pieces together tightly.

To hide the screws, add dowels to all the screw holes. Pop a little glue in each hole and push or lightly hammer in the dowels, then cut them flush with a handsaw. You can pare off any small edges of dowel by holding a sharp chisel flat and shaving them off gently. Repeat Steps 1 to 7 to create your second set of legs.

Step 8:
Measure and mark shelf frame

When the glue has dried on your joints and top piece, it's time to add the frame for the shelf. Lay the legs on the workbench, insides facing up. Put your pencil at the point where the bottom of your cross piece meets the vertical leg. Draw a line upward at 90 degrees, and mark 20 mm (0.78 in) off it.

Step 9:
Secure shelf frame

Join the 1 m (3.3 ft) piece up to the lines you've just drawn and screw in through the side to connect everything up. Again, start with guide holes to prevent the wood splitting. Repeat Steps 8 and 9 for the other side until you have a frame that can stand up. You'll see the shape of the clothes rail coming together now.

Step 10:
Plane hanger rail

Take your 20 mm x 30 mm (0.78 in x 1.18 in) timber. Hold or clamp to your workbench and plane the edges at an angle to round them off for the hangers.

Step 11:
Attach hanger rail

To fix on your rail, draw a centre line at the top of each leg and mark where to drill. When you're happy with the placement go ahead and screw the rail on. This should secure the stand even more, leaving you with a fairly sturdy frame.

Step 12:
Mark and cut shelf edges

Now moving on to the shelf. Cut your first length of the remaining 20 mm x 45 mm (0.78 x 1.77 in) oak to go on the frame and butt it right up to the end. Using a pencil, sketch out where you need to cut so that the wood fits around the legs, then use your saw to cut out these pieces. This shape will then fit perfectly in between the legs and right up to the outside edge of the frame.

Step 13: Cut slats

At this point you can decide how you want your shelf to look. You can either go for no gaps, small gaps or large gaps. I opted for small gaps purely because I like the look of them. I spaced each piece of wood about 5 mm (0.19 in) apart.

Cut the number of lengths you need for your shelf and lay them along the frame. Clamp a straight edge to the front of your shelf, so you can push all the pieces of wood right up to it and make a perfectly straight line right along the front of the shelf.

Step 14: Nail slats

Carefully lift each slat up and add a dab of glue underneath, then hammer some fine nails through the slat and into the frame to hold everything in place. Be sure to use nails with really small heads so that they're easy to cover up with wood filler.

Step 15: Fill and finish

Just using your finger, press a little bit of filler over each nail head and wait for it to set. When the filler has dried, go over the whole shelf with a sander to smooth any snags. Sand over the rest of the clothes rail, too, to clean up any imperfections or dowels that aren't quite flush.

Project
15.
Steam box
and lamp

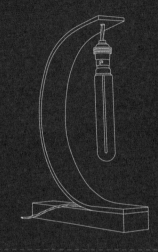

For this project, we're going to use a technique called steam bending. Although this is an incredibly old technique, it's had a real resurgence recently, especially in the UK. Traditionally used in boat building and instrument making, it's now more commonly seen in home furniture and decor.

Tools & Materials

Tools:

- Wallpaper steamer
- Clamps
- Saw
- Drill
- 16 mm (0.62 in) drill bit
- 10 mm (0.39 in) drill bit
- Basic door hinges x 2
- Small screwdriver (flat head)
- Tape measure
- Straight edge
- Sander
- Wood glue

Materials:

- 9 m (30 ft) of pine 220 mm x 20 mm (8.66 in x 0.78 in)
- 4 or 5 lengths (in case of breakages)10 mm x 65 mm x 600 mm (0.39 in x 2.55 in x 23.6 in) of straight grain oak or ash for bending
- 1 length 65 mm x 50 mm x 200 mm (2.55 in x 1.96 in x 7.87 in) of the same timber for the lamp base
- 2 m (6.5 ft) of 16 mm (0.62 in) dowel rod
- Light bulb holder
- Light bulb
- Traditional three-cord fabric flex
- Plug

Step 1:
Making the steam box

1a: Measure and cut lengths

Steam boxes aren't available to buy, so in this project we're going to go through the stages of making the steam box, the mould, and then finally the lamp. For more information on the steam bending process, head to the resources section.

Take your long pine lengths, and measure and cut them to size. I'm cutting mine to 2 m (6.5 ft) long, which means I'll make a box with plenty of space to steam longer pieces for future projects.

I'm using my chop saw to cut the wood. It has a pretty big reach on it so I can cut wide boards accurately and also a lot more efficiently. Like I mentioned in the bookshelf project on p124, chop saws are really easy to pick up for a good price these days and they're a great tool to have around in the workshop to make your life easier.

1b:
Mark lengths

Select two of your long pine lengths for the sides of the box and, using a pencil and tape, measure 140 mm (5.51 in) down the length of both pieces. Then using a straight edge, draw a line down the whole length of your timbers.

1c:
Mark and drill dowel holes

Take the first timber and make marks every 200 mm (8 in) along the lines you drew. Then, taking a drill bit the same diameter as your dowel rod, drill holes on each mark.

When your steam box is all put together, these holes will hold the dowels that will form a shelf inside your box for your lengths of timber to sit on. Having a shelf will prevent the wood from just sitting on the bottom of the box and allow the steam to fully surround it.

1d:
Cut and insert dowel rods

Cut your dowel rods to 220 mm (8.66 in), or the same width as your timber, then carefully push or hammer them into the holes you just drilled. Be really careful not to split the dowel or even the pine at this stage.

Take your second length of timber and mark it every 200 mm (8 in) as in Step 1C. Drill your holes, being careful to line them up with the dowels on your first timber.

1e:
Cut side and end pieces

Measure and cut two more long pine lengths to make two more sides for your steam box. Then measure and cut two smaller pieces to fit on each end of your box.

1f:
Assemble steam box

Now you can start putting your box together. Lay the dowelled sides facing each other and slot them together. Then screw the top and bottom sides of the box onto the dowelled sides.

Next screw the end piece on. Take your drill and drill a hole nice and central on this end piece, approximately the same size as your steamer pipe. You can also drill a small hole underneath, on the bottom of your box – this ensures the pressure doesn't build up while you're using the steam box, and also allows any water to drip out. It's highly unlikely that it'll become pressurized, but it's best to take precautions.

1g: Screw hinges

Add your hinges to the front "door" bit of wood (the other end piece) and screw them to the side of your box. These don't need to be particularly neat, but it's important that the door has a nice, tight fit.

1h: Prepare steamer

Put your box on a sturdy base outside, or in a well ventilated area, and push your steamer pipe through the hole you drilled in the back in Step 1F. I also ended up screwing an offcut to the side and to the door of the box so that I could clamp the door shut to keep the steam in. Fill your steamer with water, plug it in and wait for it to warm up. This may take a few minutes.

1i: Steam wood

When your box is full of steam, pop in your piece of oak or ash, and clamp the door shut. I kept the door shut and allowed the wood to steam for at least two hours. Online it suggests steaming for one hour per 25 mm (1 in) of thickness, regardless of the width – bear this in mind, but also test things out yourself.

Tip:

This was the first time I've ever tried to steam-bend wood, so I spent a lot of time online reading up as much as possible and asking trusted friends who had done it before. I think there's a lot of trial and error involved in the first few goes at this, so be sure to have four or five lengths of timber to bend, and be prepared to have a few of them snap on you.

Step 2:
Making the form and bending the timber

While you're waiting for your wood to steam in the steam box you can go ahead and make the form – your template shape .

2a: Mark and cut form

I'd like my lamp to be bent to a "C" shape, so I drew around an old wheel onto some old timber with a similar thickness to the wood in my steamer. Alternatively you could use a pair of compasses to draw a circle.

It's a good idea to overcompensate when it comes to any shape you're cutting – here I'm making it the circle tighter – to allow for the wood to spring back when unclamping.

Use a jigsaw to cut out the shape, and also cut out a couple of notches on the opposite side for your clamps to sit in when it comes to bending.

2b: Check and secure form

Screw your form shape onto a solid base like a workbench or flat slab of wood. At this point it's important to check that all your clamps fit around your form. This could save some potential issues later on.

2c: Clamp steamed wood

After the necessary time, take your wood out of the steamer. Be very careful not to be scalded as you open the door – the steam has been building up for a few hours, so there will be a cloud of steam released as soon as you open it.

Wear a thick pair of gloves to remove your piece of wood and clamp it onto the form as quickly as you can. I mentioned earlier that it may take a few goes to get this right, so be patient and persistent when it comes to the bending stage. When it works out, it's a very exciting and fun moment.

Leave your wood on the form for at least 72 hours to allow it to fully dry out again.

Step 3:
Making the lamp

3a: Unclamp and sand wood

Unclamp your wood after the required amount of time and pass over it with some sandpaper, to soften the edges and give it a clean up.

3b: Measure and drill flex hole

Make a mark at the top of your lamp, measuring it carefully to ensure it's nice and central. Then drill a 10 mm (0.39 in) hole for the flex to go through.

3c: Glue and clamp wood

Add some glue to your base piece, where your curved wood is going to sit, and clamp your bent piece in place.

3d: Wire plug

While the glue is drying you can start putting the electrics together. Be really aware of what you're doing here and be sure to stick to the diagrams on the plug, or check online to make sure you're doing it right. Alternatively you can ask an electrician to do this for you.

3e:
Connect bulb holder

Thread your cable through the hole you drilled in the top and connect your bulb holder to the cable, again being careful to ensure the correct cables are going in the correct places.

3f: Fit bulb

Fit your bulb and plug your cable in to make sure everything works. I pulled my cable tight, then tucked it in between the curved timber and the base to keep it nice and tight along the back of the lamp.

Resources

All the tools and materials used throughout the book are readily available in most DIY and hardware stores, or online. Here's a short list of places they can be found and also some websites and makers you may find helpful paired with a couple of the projects in the book.

Tools

Axeminster Tools & Machinery
www.axeminster.co.uk

Makita Tools
www.makitauk.com

Amazon
www.amazon.co.uk

Useful information

Steam bending // www.leevalley.com/us/html/05F1501ie.pdf // en.wikipedia.org/wiki/Steam_bending

Making 'wood butter' finish for spoons and chopping boards // www.theprairiehomestead.com/2018/01/home-made-spoon-butter-recipe.html

Makers

Weaving // Christabel Balfour – @Christabelbalfour, www.christabelbalfour.com.

Steam bending // Tom Raffield – www.tomraffield.com, @tomraffield.

Other // Instagram: @hopeinthewoods, @grainandknot, @aesoderlund, @artbrugi, @commonwoodwork, @brian_christopher, @1924us, @alephgeddis, @theportlandstudio

Shopping

Arkonaplatz flea market: Berlin, Germany

Baileys Home: Bridstow, UK // @baileyshome, www.baileyshome.com

Hay House: Copenhagen, Denmark // @haydesign, hay.dk

Labour and Wait: London, UK // @baileyshome, www.labourandwait.co.uk

Objects of Use: Oxford, UK // @objectsofuse, www.objectsofuse.com

The Union Project: Cheltenham, UK // @designandhomestore, www.theunionproject.co.uk

La Trésorerie: Paris, France // @baileyshome, www.latresorerie.fr

Outro

It's been such an amazing privilege to have the opportunity to write a book to help people on their making journey, particularly in working with wood. I'm so excited for each reader to discover the joy that woodworking brings for the first time and I'm excited to see where your making takes you. I hope that you've felt inspired as you've read through the book, and that as you've worked through each project your confidence has grown. When doing anything practical I believe that having the space for trial and error is really important. Having an opportunity to experiment with new materials, tools and techniques is such a joy and shouldn't be rushed. Take everything in, enjoy it, and use your hands and your mind to learn in a totally new and different way.

As for the 15 projects you've just read through, I encourage you to experiment as much as you feel comfortable. Make things at different sizes, try new materials, do whatever it takes to create a totally unique and functional piece that suits you and your lifestyle. Enjoy the item being used and worn in, slowly becoming a piece that, without intention, is an essential part of your everyday life.

This project wouldn't have ever happened without the help of Issy and the amazing team at Carlton Books, thanks for giving me a shot! Thank you to some amazing friends -- Emily, Maddie, Isaac, Ollie, Lilly, Mike (to name just a few), who have blessed me beyond belief in past years and especially through this. Thank you for your encouragement and the positivity you've spoken over me and my business for the last few years. For the prayers and messages I've received over the last few months while writing the book. For the coffees that have been bought to keep me going through some long days!

The Troughton Family, for blessing me with the space to grow my business into more than just a hobby. Thank you for the workshop space you provided. Without the barn it's unlikely this would all be happening.

My family, who I can't thank enough for everything. My grandparents who have encouraged me and spurred me toward doing something I love. My brother, Olly, for your love and encouragement. Your weekly phone calls checking in, and the kind words you continue to speak over me and my business. Mum and Dad, your wisdom and words of advice, your amazing patience and love you've given have been real blessings over the years. It's been difficult, and there've been a lot of doubts and struggles, but thank you for always pushing me forward and encouraging me in all I do.

To my amazing God, who I get to worship through my business, not my business success.

Tobias George

Tobias George
@tobgam
www.tobiasgeorge.com
info@tobiasgeorge.com

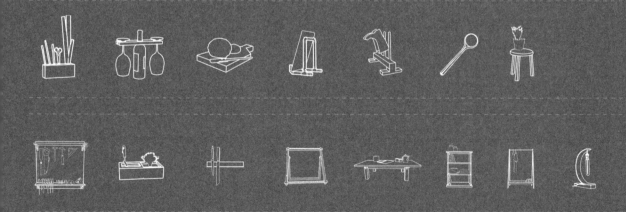